Take Your (Equally Horible) Pick!

TAKE YOUR PICK OF

DISGUSTING FOODS

BY G.G. LAKE

CAPSTONE PRESS
a capstone imprint

Blazers Books are published by Capstone Press,
1710 Roe Crest Drive, North Mankato, Minnesota 56003
www.mycapstone.com

Library of Congress Cataloging-in-Publication Data
Cataloging-in-publication data is available on the Library of Congress website.
ISBN 978-1-5157-4470-2 (library binding)
ISBN 978-1-5157-4474-0 (paperback)
ISBN 978-1-5157-4486-3 (eBook PDF)

Think of the grossest foods ever and pick which one you're going to eat! Tarantulas, cow's blood,
head cheese—which sounds tastiest to you?

Editorial Credits
Nikki Potts, editor; Kyle Grenz, designer; Tracey Engel, media researcher;
Kathy McColley, production specialist

Photo Credits
Alamy: Kyndell Harkness/Minneapolis Star Tribune/ZUMA Wire, 10; Dreamstime: Lauri Dammert,
15; Getty Images: Tobias Titz, 14; iStockphoto: Chalabala, 13, h3ct02, 20 Left, master1305, 6, NZSteve,
12, Robin O'Connell, 23; Newscom: REUTERS/Toshi Maeda, 17; Shutterstock: Alexander Schuessel,
19, D. Kucharski K. Kucharska, 5, Dar1930, 25, DD Images, front cover (bottom), Fanfo, 27, iTons, 24,
kps123, 16, Mintra Chumpoosueb, 8, Moolkum, 7, Rafal Cichawa, 20–21, Sam Dcruz, 11, siriratt, 9,
successo images, 22, Vladiczech, back cover and spine, Vova Shevchuk, front cover (top), vvoe, 26;
Wikimedia Commons: CC-BY-SA-2.5/Shardan, 18

Printed and bound in China.
007887

TABLE OF CONTENTS

PICKY EATERS BEWARE!

The type of food you eat often depends on where you live. Would you eat grasshoppers? They're a popular food in Mexico. What if all you had to eat were disgusting foods? Which would you pick?

COW'S BLOOD OR KOPI LUWAK COFFEE

Would you drink cow's blood or Kopi Luwak coffee?

COW'S BLOOD
DRANK IN: KENYA AND TANZANIA

► People either drink the blood by itself or mix it with milk.

► Sometimes people drink the blood straight from the cow's neck with a straw.

► The cow is kept alive throughout this process.

KOPI LUWAK COFFEE

DRANK IN: SOUTHEAST ASIA

► Asian palm **civets** eat coffee cherries. When the civets poop out the cherries, coffee makers turn the droppings into Kopi Luwak coffee.

► The coffee tastes smooth, fruity, and a little like chocolate.

► Careful! Coffee made from old droppings can make you sick.

civet droppings

civet—a catlike animal found in southern parts of Asia

FOIE GRAS OR TRIPE

Would you eat foie gras or tripe?

FOIE GRAS
EATEN IN: FRANCE

WHAT IS IT? A FAT LIVER FROM A DUCK OR GOOSE

- ► The meal can be eaten hot or cold.

- ► Foie gras has a creamy and buttery taste.

- ► Foie gras can be deadly. Eating it regularly can cause life-threatening **diseases**.

disease—a sickness or illness

TRIPE

▶ In the United Kingdom, tripe is **bleached** and boiled before it's eaten.

▶ Tripe starts to feel like a sponge if it's cooked for a long time.

▶ Tripe doesn't have much of a taste. But it's very chewy.

bleach—to make something cleaner by soaking it in a chemical

LUTEFISK OR GOAT'S HEAD

Would you rather eat lutefisk or goat's head?

LUTEFISK

EATEN IN: MIDWESTERN UNITED STATES; SOME PARTS OF NORWAY

- ► The fish is dried until it turns leathery. Then the fish is soaked in water and **lye** for many days.

- ► Lutefisk looks like white Jell-O and smells awful.

- ► Some people say lutefisk can break down silver.

lye—a strong chemical often used for making soap

GOAT'S HEAD
EATEN IN: NIGERIA

► The tongue, ears, and brain are cooked separately. The eyes are cooked in the head.

► The guest of honor eats the eyes. He or she uses a fork to remove them from the skull.

► Fans of this food say the eyes and ears are best if eaten warm.

TARANTULA OR SCORPION

Would you eat a tarantula or a scorpion?

TARANTULA

EATEN IN: CAMBODIA

▶ Tarantulas are deep-fried with salt, sugar, and garlic.

▶ The meal has a crunchy outside and a gooey inside.

▶ You can eat them whole or bite one leg off at a time.

SCORPION

EATEN IN: CHINA

▶ Street vendors either roast scorpions or fry them.

▶ Fried scorpions have an oily flavor with a bit of a crunch.

▶ Roasted scorpions have a fishy taste.

WITCHETTY GRUB
OR MOPANE WORM

Would you rather eat a witchetty grub or a mopane worm?

WITCHETTY GRUB
EATEN IN: AUSTRALIA

► Witchetty grubs are usually grilled over a fire.

► Sometimes the grubs are swallowed whole while they're still alive.

► Witchetty grubs have a nutty flavor.

MOPANE WORM

EATEN IN: SOUTHERN AFRICA

► The worm can be fried, put into a stew, or roasted over a fire.

► Fried worms are usually cooked with onions and tomato sauce.

► Sometimes mopane worms are dried out under the hot sun. Sun-dried worms taste a little like potato chips.

NATTO OR JIBACHI SENBEI

Would you pick natto or jibachi senbei to chew?

NATTO

EATEN IN: JAPAN

WHAT IS IT? NATTO IS MADE OF FERMENTED SOYBEANS

► Natto's smell is so strong that it can make people sick.

► Natto is covered in a sticky, gooey substance. This substance hangs in strings. Strings of the goo can get up to 4 feet (1.2 meters) long.

► Some people try to hide natto's taste with mustard or soy sauce.

ferment—to undergo a chemical change caused by bacteria

JIBACHI SENBEI

EATEN IN: OMACHI, JAPAN
WHAT IS IT? A RICE CRACKER WITH DIGGER WASPS MIXED IN

► Digger wasps are boiled before going into the cracker.

► Each cracker is full of wasps.

► The sweet cracker masks the bitter taste of wasp. But the cracker doesn't hide the feel of a wing on your tongue as you chew!

CASU MARZU
OR HÁKARL

Would you choose casu marzu or hákarl?

CASU MARZU
EATEN IN: SARDINA

▶ Makers allow a fly to lay eggs inside a wheel of cheese. Once the eggs hatch, **maggots** slowly start to eat the cheese.

▶ People eat the cheese with the live maggots in it. The maggots in the cheese can jump 6 inches (15 centimeters). They can jump right into your eyes!

▶ Eating this cheese can cause bad stomach pain and **vomiting**.

maggot—a stage of development between an egg and an adult in certain flies

vomit—to throw up food and liquid from your stomach through your mouth

18

HÁKARL

EATEN IN: ICELAND
WHAT IS IT? RAW AND ROTTEN SHARK

► The meat can be **poisonous** to humans. It has to be prepared for many months before it can be eaten.

► Hákarl stinks of **urine** and rotten fish. The smell makes first-time hákarl eaters gag.

► Some people say hákarl tastes like old cheese.

poisonous—able to kill or harm if swallowed, inhaled, or sometimes even touched

urine—a body's liquid waste

BALUT or CUY

Would you pick balut or cuy?

BALUT

EATEN IN: PHILIPPINES

WHAT IS IT? A HARD-BOILED EGG WITH A HALF-FORMED BABY DUCK INSIDE

▶ The head of the unborn duck has a creamy quality.

▶ Everything except the shell is on the menu. In some cases bones, feathers, and beaks are present.

▶ The bird's partially-developed bones are soft enough to chew and swallow.

CUY

WHAT IS IT? A GUINEA PIG FOUND IN SOUTH AMERICA

► Cuy is often roasted over a fire. But it also can be barbecued or deep-fried.

► The whole animal is cooked, including the head.

► The taste is similar to wild pheasant.

SANNAKJI
OR MUKTUK

Would you eat an octopus or whale blubber?

SANNAKJI

EATEN IN: KOREA

WHAT IS IT? A SMALL, LIVE OCTOPUS

▶ The octopus is cut up while it's still alive.

▶ The **tentacles** are separate but still moving. The head of the octopus is put on the plate, in case you'd like to eat that too.

▶ The suction cups on the tentacles stick to everything. They will even get caught in your throat. For this reason, eating sannakji is a serious choking hazard.

tentacle—a long, armlike body part some animals use to touch, grab, or smell

MUKTUK

EATEN IN: ALASKA, NORTHERN CANADA

▶ A whale's outer layer of skin and **blubber** are cut and sliced. The meat is usually sprinkled with salt before being eaten raw.

▶ Some people say muktuk tastes like scrambled eggs.

▶ Muktuk is risky to eat. People can get food poisoning from eating it.

blubber—a thick layer of fat underneath the skin of some animals

BIRD'S NEST SOUP
OR SVARTSOPPA

Would you rather have bird's nest soup or goose blood soup?

BIRD'S NEST SOUP
EATEN IN: PHILIPPINES AND CHINA

► Swiftlet nests are used for this soup. These birds make their nests with their own saliva. So this soup is actually made from bird spit!

► Bird's nest soup doesn't have much of a taste, except for a hint of sugar.

► Some people claim the soup helps fight aging and **cancer**.

cancer—a disease in which some cells in the body grow faster than normal cells

24

SVARTSOPPA

EATEN IN: SWEDEN
WHAT IS IT?
GOOSE BLOOD SOUP

▶ The blood soup is thick and is red-black in color. It looks like blood-colored gravy.

▶ It contains small pieces of heart, **gizzard**, neck, and wing tips.

▶ The soup tastes both sweet and sour.

gizzard—the part of the bird's stomach that is used for crushing food

HEAD CHEESE OR KHASH

Would you pick head cheese or khash?

HEAD CHEESE
EATEN IN: EUROPE

► There's nothing cheesy about head cheese. It's the cooked down meat and fat from the head of a cow or a pig.

► The meat and fat are pressed into a mold. **Gelatin** is added to keep everything together.

► Many people eat head cheese in slices on a sandwich.

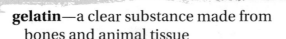

gelatin—a clear substance made from bones and animal tissue

KHASH

EATEN IN: ARMENIA

► A cow's head, stomach lining, and feet all float in khash.

► Khash is cooked for so long that meat falls off the bones. But the bones still float in the soup pot!

► No spoons are needed. Khash is eaten with your hands and hardened bread!

RAPID ROUND

Which of these would you NEVER eat?
CASU MARZU OR LUTEFISK ?

Which would be better at breakfast?
NATTO OR MUKTUK ?

Which would you make
your family for dinner?
KHASH OR CUY ?

Which would you pick for
flavored chewing gum?
COW'S BLOOD OR HÁKARL ?

Which would you have
on a cold winter's night?
SVARTSOPPA OR TRIPE ?

Which would you eat at a fair?
TARANTULA OR MOPANE WORMS ?

Which would you pick for lunch
on summer vacation?
JIBACHI SENBEI OR SCORPION ?

Which would be more disgusting to cook?
GOAT'S HEAD OR HEAD CHEESE ?

If you were opening a restaurant,
which would you serve?
WITCHETTY GRUB OR BALUT ?

Which ingredient would you gather?
CIVET POOP OR SWIFTLET NESTS ?

GLOSSARY

bleach (BLEECH)—to make something cleaner by soaking it in a chemical

blubber (BLUH-buhr)—a thick layer of fat underneath the skin of some animals

cancer (KAN-suhr)—a disease in which some cells in the body grow faster than normal cells

civet (SIV-et)—a catlike animal found in southern parts of Asia

disease (di-ZEEZ)—a sickness or illness

ferment (fur-MENT)—to undergo a chemical change caused by bacteria

gelatin (JEL-uh-tuhn)—a clear substance made from bones and animal tissue

gizzard (GIZ-erd)—the part of the bird's stomach that is used for crushing food

lye (LYE)—a strong chemical often used for making soap

maggot (MAG-uht)—a stage of development between an egg and an adult in certain flies

poisonous (POI-zuhn-uhss)—able to kill or harm if swallowed, inhaled, or sometimes even touched

tentacle (TEN-tuh-kuhl)—a long, armlike body part some animals use to touch, grab, or smell

urine (YOOR-uhn)—a body's liquid waste

vomit (VOM-it)—to throw up food and liquid from your stomach through your mouth

READ MORE

Klepeis, Alicia. *The World's Strangest Foods.* Library of Weird. Mankato, Minn.: Capstone Press, 2015.

Loewen, Nancy and Paula Skelley. *Food of the World.* Go Go Global. North Mankato, Minn.: Capstone Press, 2015.

Perish, Patrick. *Disgusting Foods.* Totally Disgusting. Minneapolis: Bellwether Media, 2015.

INTERNET SITES

FactHound offers a safe, fun way to find Internet sites related to this book. All of the sites on FactHound have been researched by our staff.

Here's all you do:

Visit *www.facthound.com*

Type in this code: 9781515744702

Super-cool stuff!

Check out projects, games and lots more at
www.capstonekids.com

INDEX